Happy Baptism Day

Happy Baptism Day

by
Judy Jolly

Illustrated by
Susan Harrison

Abingdon Press

HAPPY BAPTISM DAY

ISBN 0-687-03064-1

Library of Congress Cataloging-in-Publication Data
for HAPPY BAPTISM DAY
is available from the Library of Congress.

02 03 04 05 06 07 08 09 10 11—10 9 8 7 6 5 4 3 2 1

PRINTED IN HONG KONG

This book is presented to

____

By ______________________________

On ______________________________

"Time for bed," Mom called.

Anna Lois pretended that she didn't hear Mom. Anna Lois pretended, but just for a minute. Then Anna Lois remembered. Today is Anna Lois's

"Happy Baptism Day."

"Coming, Mom," Anna Lois called, as she began putting away her markers, paper, and stickers.

Mom helped Anna Lois put on her favorite pajamas. Mom searched for Anna Lois's stuffed cat. Anna Lois brushed her teeth and her hair.

"I don't want a snack tonight, Mom," Anna Lois announced. "I'm still not hungry." Anna Lois smiled when she thought about the "Baptism Feast" that the family had enjoyed after worship that day. Grandmother, Uncle Joe, and some of her family's best friends had joined her family for Sunday dinner, Anna Lois's Happy Baptism Day Feast. They all had eaten too much, but the food tasted so good. Now that it was bedtime, Anna Lois still did not want another bite.

"Where did you see God today?" Mom asked as she tucked the covers under Anna Lois's chin. "Oh!" thought Anna Lois, "God was in the sanctuary when Samuel and I were baptized. And God rode home with us when we talked about our mission trip to play with the mountain children at their Bible school. And God was at our Happy Baptism Day Feast when we asked God to bless our food and help us remember this special day. God was with us when we lighted the baptism candles for Samuel and for me."

It had been a special day and a special week for Anna Lois. All week long her family had talked about the worship service at her church. They had met with Reverend Patrick, one of their pastors, to practice what they would say and what they would do at the Baptismal Covenant service. They had practiced sitting on the first pew close to the front of the sanctuary. They had practiced standing at the altar rail, close to the baptismal font. They had practiced kneeling while Reverend Patrick placed his hands first on Anna Lois's head, then on Samuel's head.

On that Wednesday afternoon when they practiced, Reverend Patrick had asked Anna Lois and Samuel if they wanted to look at the water in the baptismal font. The bowl that held the water was shaped like a seashell. The shell reminded Anna Lois of the one she had saved from their trip to the beach last summer. And the shell looked like the one that Mr. Phillips, Anna Lois's Sunday school teacher, had given her on her Happy Baptism Day.

When they practiced, Reverend Patrick had told Anna Lois, "Your church family will welcome you, Anna Lois. They will welcome Samuel, too. You, Samuel, and I will walk up the aisle and the congregation will sing a song that you know. You may sing, too, if you would like. I will give your mom a special baptismal certificate and the special baptismal candle that we will have lighted. You may save these forever in a special place to remember your Happy Baptism Day."

On Anna Lois's Happy Baptism Day, Mr. Phillips, her Sunday school teacher, had talked about Anna Lois's special day. Mr. Phillips had talked about God's love. Mr. Phillips had even shared the Bible story that he knew was Anna Lois's favorite. "Water is a special part of baptism," Mr. Phillips had told the class.

All week long Mom, Samuel, and Anna Lois had shared Bible stories about water. Anna Lois's favorite was the story about Noah and all the animals on the ark. Samuel loved animals so he enjoyed hearing about Noah, too. On the night of Anna Lois's Happy Baptism Day, Mom agreed to tell the Noah's ark story again.

"Noah loved God," Mom began. "Noah listened to God and Noah obeyed God."

Mom talked about the days and days of rain. She let the children name the animals that they imagined on the ark. They wondered how everyone got along. They wondered how there was enough food to go around. Then they got to Anna Lois's favorite part. "And Noah opened the window and let the bird back in. The bird was carrying a branch from the earth," Mom said. "And Noah knew that they were safe," added Anna Lois. Samuel cheered. "Hooray!" And Anna Lois smiled. It had been a wonderful Happy Baptism Day.

"Thank you, Mom," said Anna Lois.

"Thank you, God," said Anna Lois, Samuel, and Mom.

"Thank you, God, for loving us. And thank you for my Happy Baptism Day."